BIBLE REBUS PUZZLES

by
Amy Daniel

Cover by Vanessa Filkins

ISBN No. 0-86653-422-9

Standardized Subject Code TA ac

Printing No. 987654

Shining Star Publications
23740 Hawthorne Boulevard
Torrance, CA 90505-5927
A Division of
Frank Schaffer Publications, Inc.

Unless otherwise indicated, the New International Version of the Bible was used in preparing the activities in this book.

DEDICATION

For Mema
with love,
Amy

TABLE OF CONTENTS

INTRODUCTION

Bible Rebus Puzzles contains forty-two rebus puzzles, based on familiar Bible verses, that will challenge puzzle enthusiasts from age 8 to adults. The New International Version of the Bible was used to create these puzzles and should be used when solving or checking Scriptures.

The exact spelling of the word is usually used if letters are added to or subtracted from a picture. There are a few exceptions for homonyms and sound-alike words. For example, him =hymn; four=for; t +(hay)=they; ½=have; NMEs=enemies.

After students solve a puzzle, have them check the answer by looking up the Scripture verse(s). If time allows, encourage children to write rebus Bible verses for Scriptures you are studying.

These puzzles are appropriate for independent use, pairs, for use by small groups, or they make delightful party games for large groups. The selected verses will motivate Scripture memory, reinforce Bible research skills and challenge imaginations and creativity in all your Bible students. The answer key on page 47 makes this book a hassle-free teaching tool. Reproducible awards on page 48 are included so you can reward exceptional effort. Have fun solving and creating rebus Bible verses.

PUZZLE #1
Matthew 10:30

 – h ______ 7 – s ______ 3 – RE ______

 – st + ry ______  + S ______ of

U + R ______  – TR ______

 – S T + E ______  – B ______

 – S + ED. ______

PUZZLE #2
Psalm 150:6

L +  – J ______

e +  – st + ryth +  – r ______

t +  ______

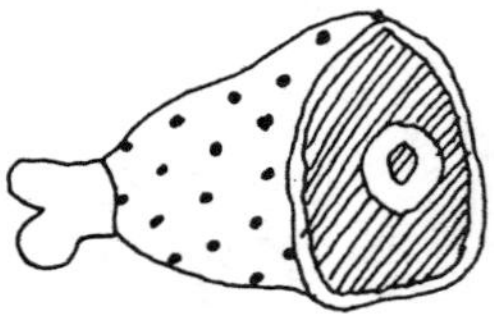 – m + s ______

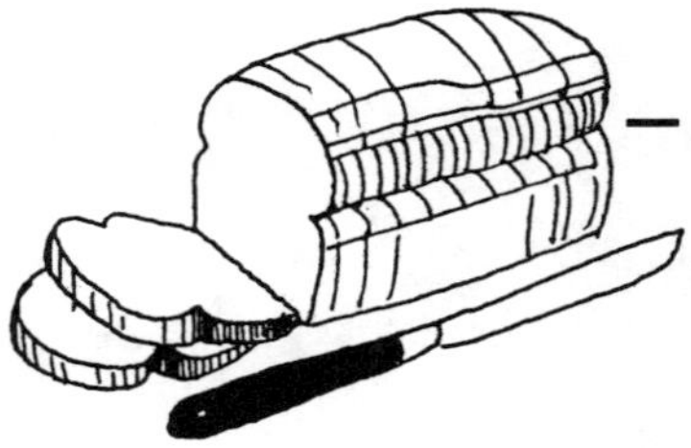 – d + th ______

P +  – tn + se ______

3 – re

______ LORD.

P +  –tn + se ______

 – rad

______ LORD.

PUZZLE #3
Hebrews 13:8

Je +  – n + s

____________ Christ

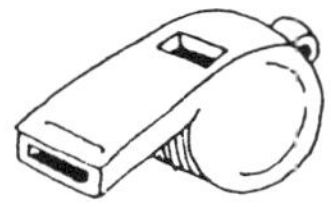 –whtle 3 –re S +  – lb + e

________ ________ ____________

y +  – v + erd +  – h

____

 – h 2 – w + d +  – h

________ ____________

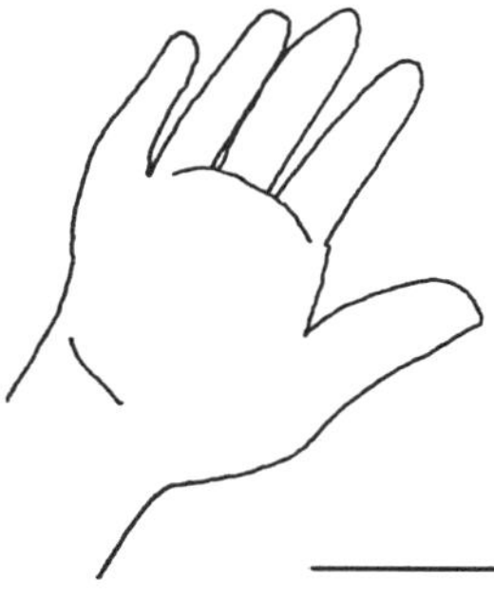 – h 4 – u + ever.

________ __________

PUZZLE #4
Matthew 7:7

"A +  – de & 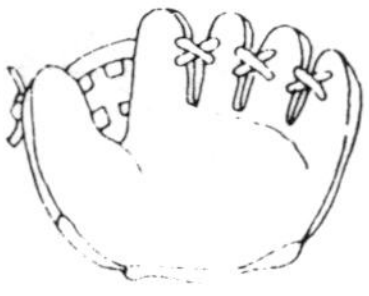 – mt

______ ______ ______

w +  – h  giv + 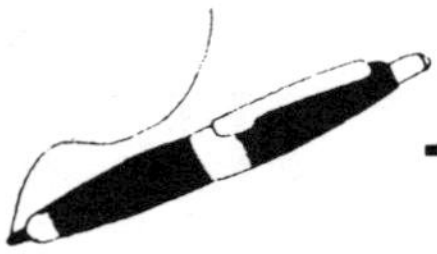 – p

______ ______ ______

2  ;  – d + k & U

______ ______ ______ ______ ______

w +  –h  – sh + nd;

______ ______

 – ee +  – bl & 3 – re

______ ______ ______ door

w +  – h  O + 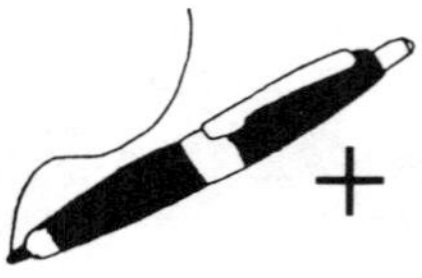 + ed 2 U."

______ ______ ______ ______ ______

PUZZLE #5
Psalm 23:6

 –n + rely  – se + d + ness

__________ __________

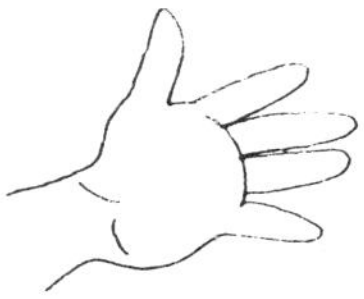 – h l +  – d w +  – h

________ __________ __________

 – n  – b 3 – re

follow ________ ________ ______

d +  – h + s m + 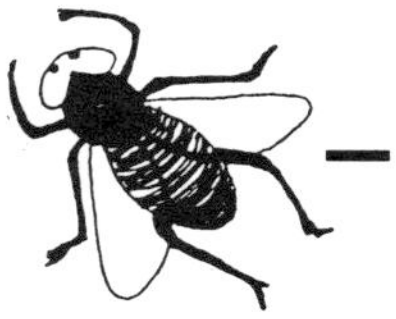 – fl  ,

__________ of ______ ________

 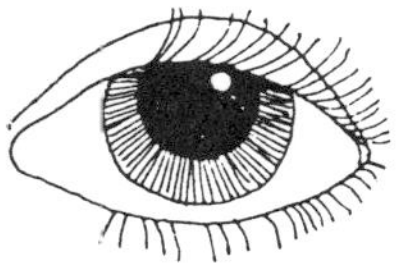 w  –h d +  N 3 – re

____ ______ ________ ________ ____ _______

 3 – re 4 – u + e+ 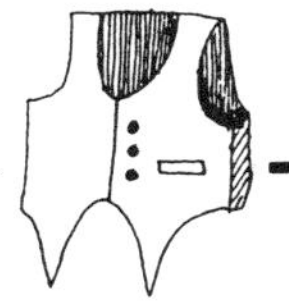 – st + r.

________ of _____ LORD ______________

PUZZLE #6
Isaiah 45:9 b

"... D +  – t **3** – re 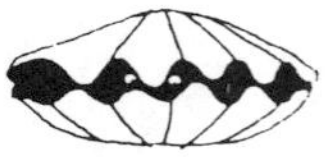 – m + y

S +  –h **2** **3**–re

 – nd + tter, 'W + 

 – c + e 

m +  – ce + 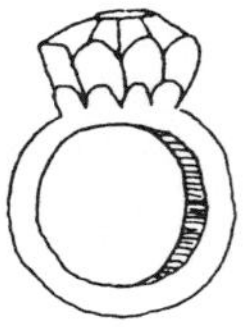 – r ? ..."'

PUZZLE #7
Jeremiah 10:10 a

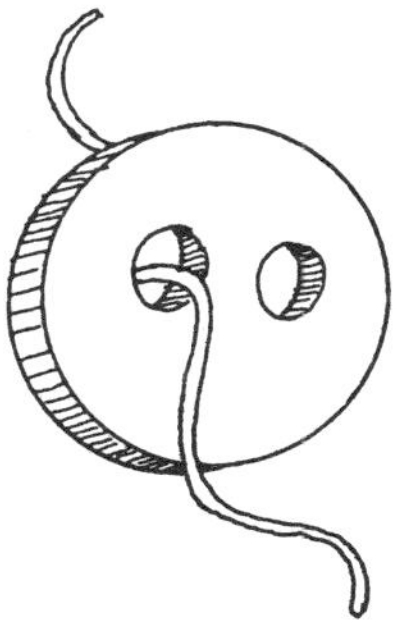 – 

3 – re

________ ________ LORD

 – fh   3 – re   t + 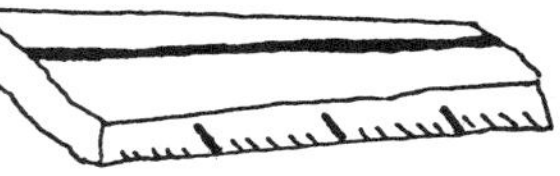 – lr

________ ________ ________

h + 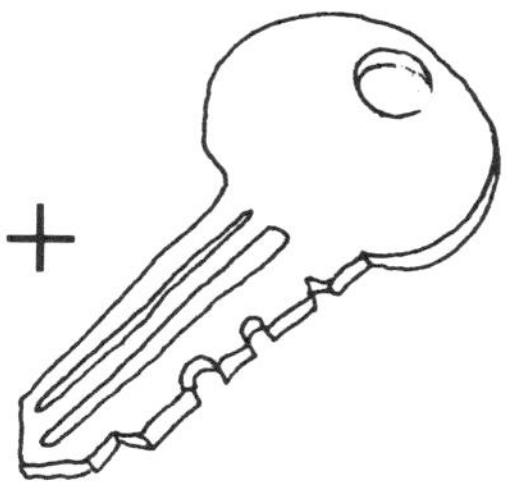 – ky   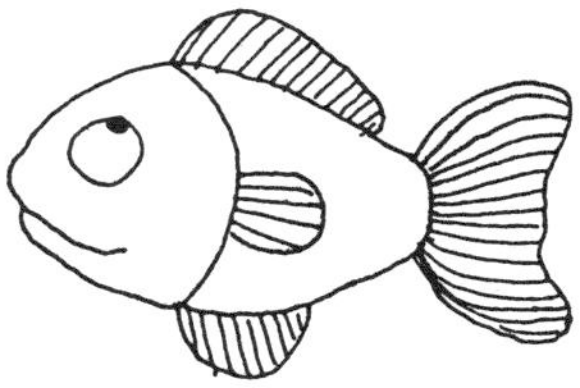 – fh

God; ________ ________

3 – re   l + 5 – fe + ing

________ ________ God,

3 – re   eter + 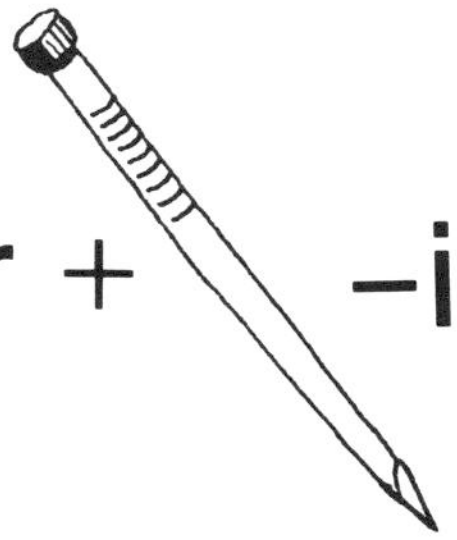 –i   .

________ ________ ________

PUZZLE #8
John 3:3

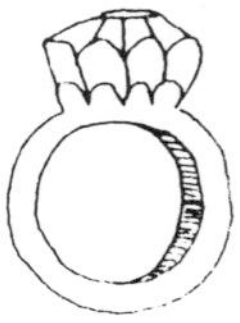 – rg ______ reply

Je +  – n + s ______

de + 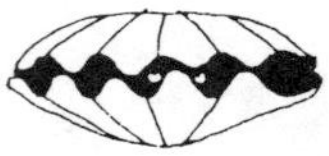 +red– m, ______

“ I

t +  – w ______

 ______

3 – re ______

 – ee + uth, ______

unless

 – cr ______

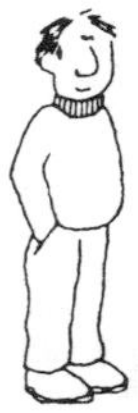 ______

 – fh ______

b +  – c ______

a + 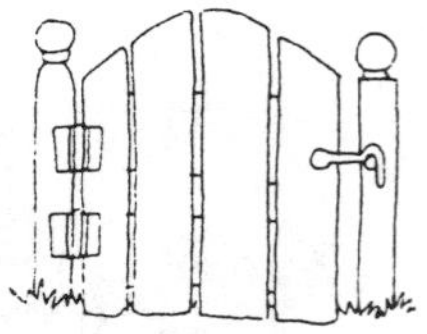 – te + in, ______

 – m ______

 +  ______

– d ______

3– re ______

 + dom ______

of God.”

PUZZLE #9
John 14:6

Je +  – n + s  – t + wered,

__________ __________

" 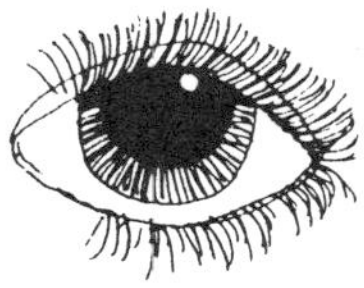 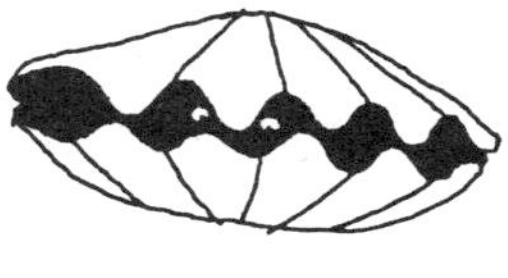 – cl **3** – re

______ ______ ______

 – hle + y & 3 – re

______ ______ ______

 – ee + uth & 3 – re  .

______ ______ ______ ______

 – se **1** 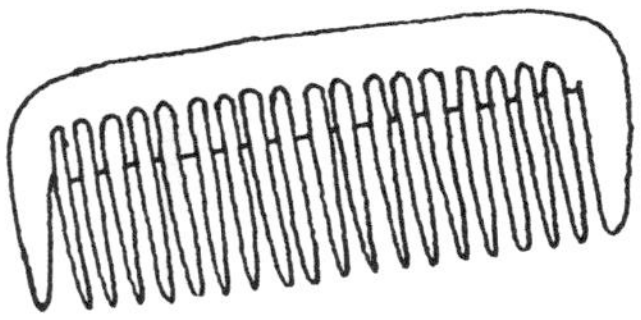 – b + es 2

______ ______ ______ ______

3 – re  –e ex + 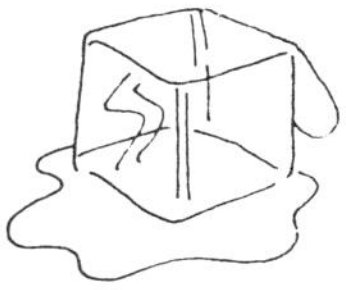 – i+ pt

______ ______ ______

3 –ee + ough  – ul."

______ ______

PUZZLE #10

John 18:36 a

Je +  – n +s "m + 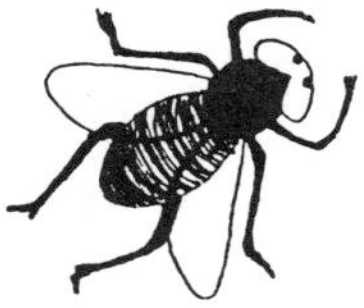 –fl

_________ said, _____

 + dom  – fh 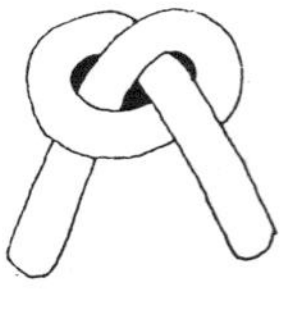 of this

_________ _____ _____

 .  – mt 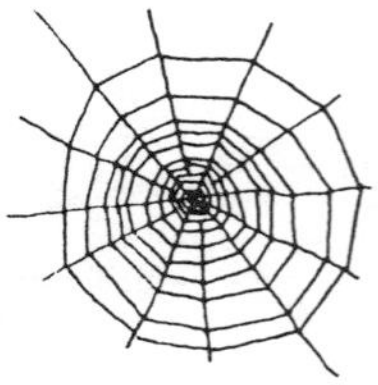 – b + re,

_______ If _____ ________

m + 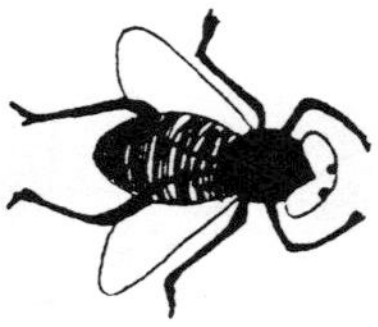 –fl serv +  would

_______ __________

f +  –n 2 pre + 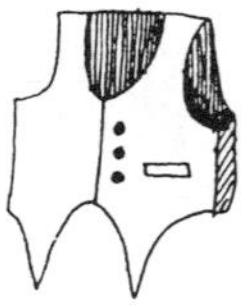 – st + nt

________ _____ ___________

m +  – fl arr +  – n

________ _________

by 3 – re Jews . . . ."

______

PUZZLE #11
Romans 6:23 b

. . . 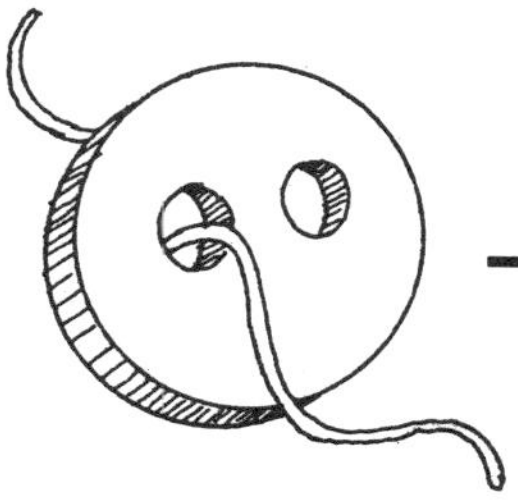 – 

______

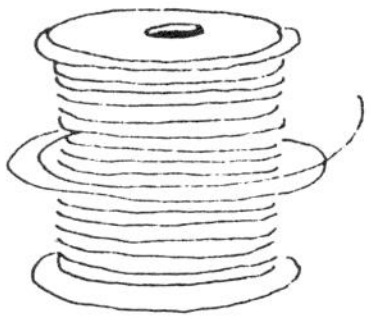 – rad

______

______ of God

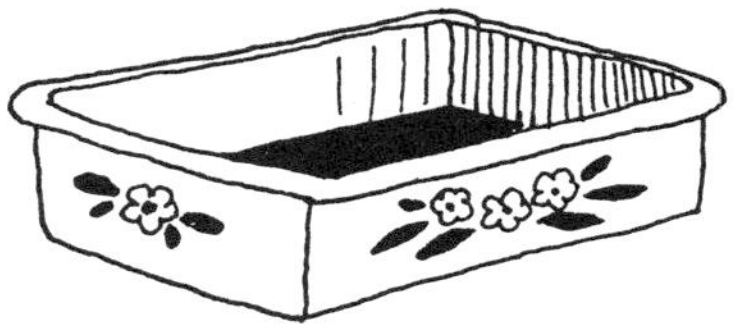 – dh

______

eter 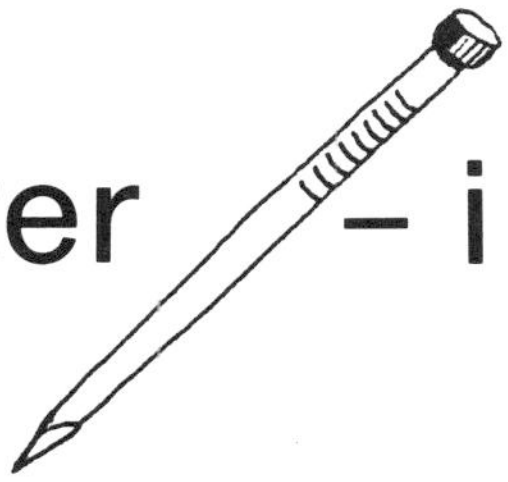 – i

______

______

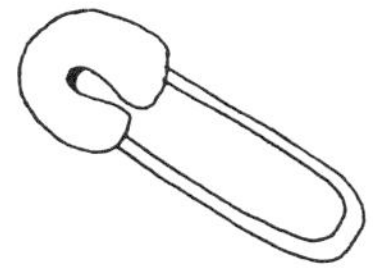 –p

______

Je +  – n + s

Christ ______

 – cld + r

______ LORD.

PUZZLE #12
Isaiah 44:6 b

. . . 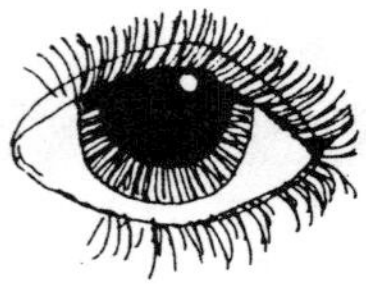 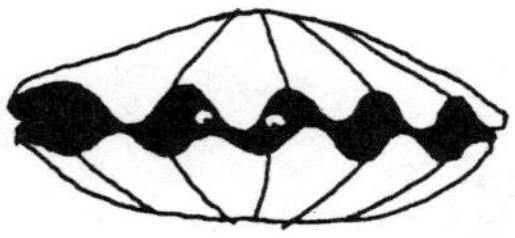 –cl 3 – re

____ ____ ____

 – e + st  –h  – pe

____ ____ ____

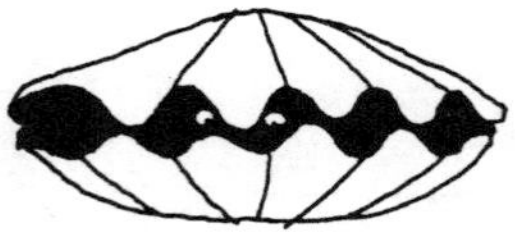 – cl 3 – re la + 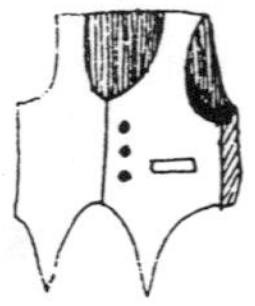 – ve;

____ ____ ____

 – e + art  – g + m

____ ____

 – ul 3 – ree + ere

____ ____

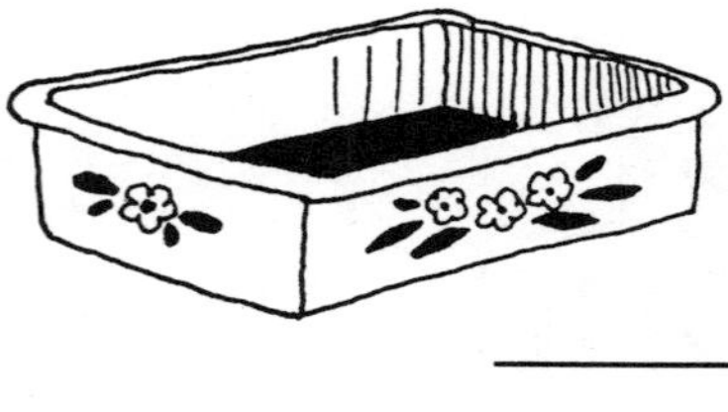 – dh  – se

____ ____ God.

PUZZLE #13
Romans 8:28

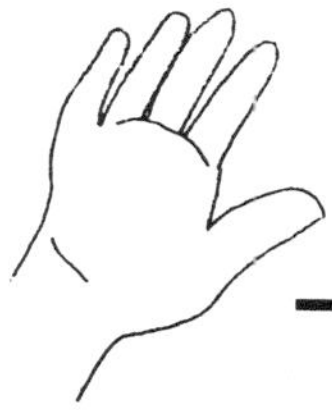 – h 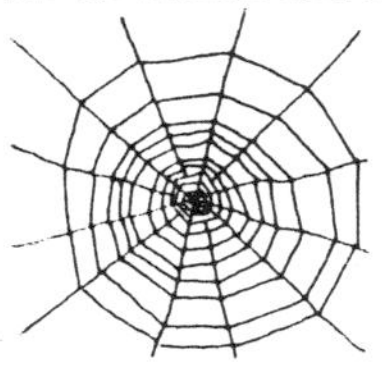 – b k +  – s

________ ________ ________

t +  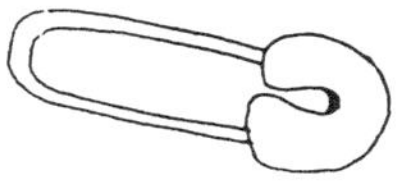 – p  – b

________ ______ ______ things

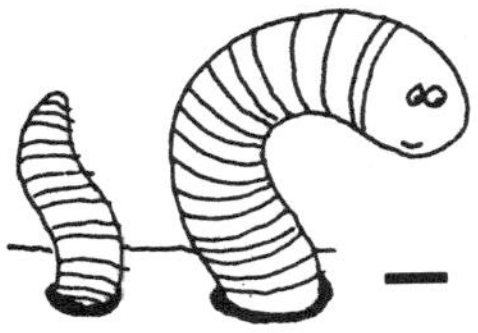 – m + ks 4  – se + d

God ________ _____ the _______

t + 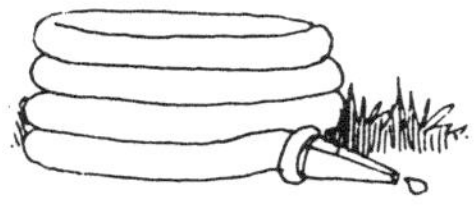 w + 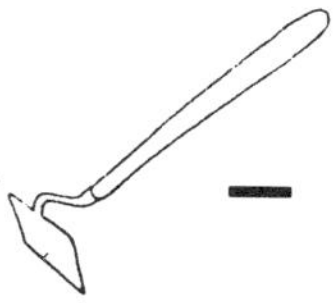 – e l +  – d

of ________ ________ ________

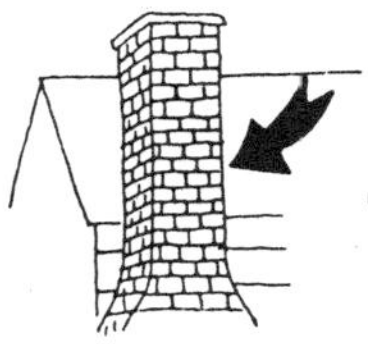 – cney, w + 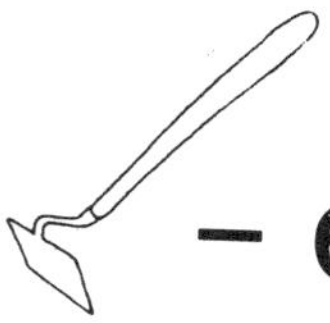 – e   + n

________ ________ ______ ______

ac + 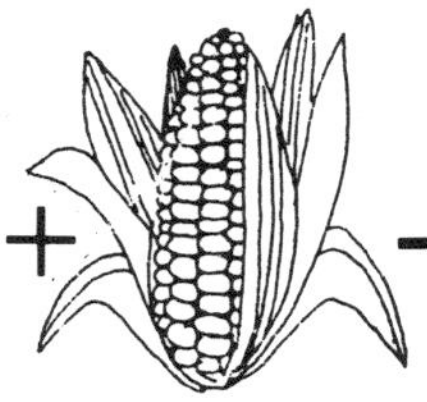 – n + ding

called ____________ to his purpose.

PUZZLE #14
Psalm 116:1

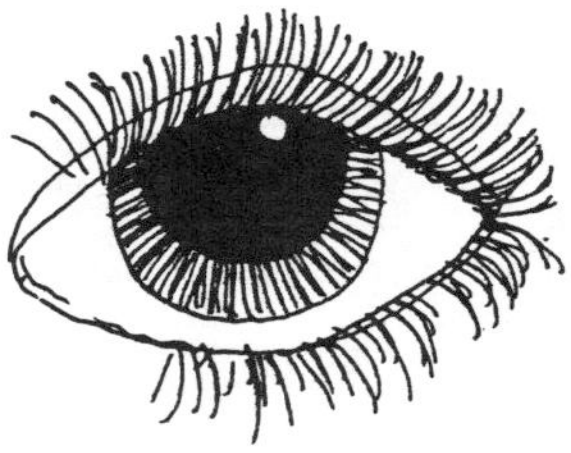

l +  – d

3 – re

______ ______ ______

4  – n

h + 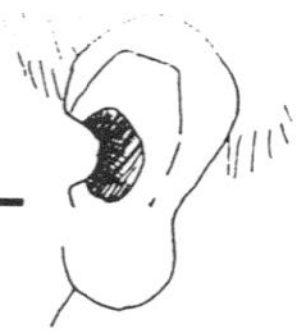 + d

LORD, ______ ______ ______

m +  – ak

vo + 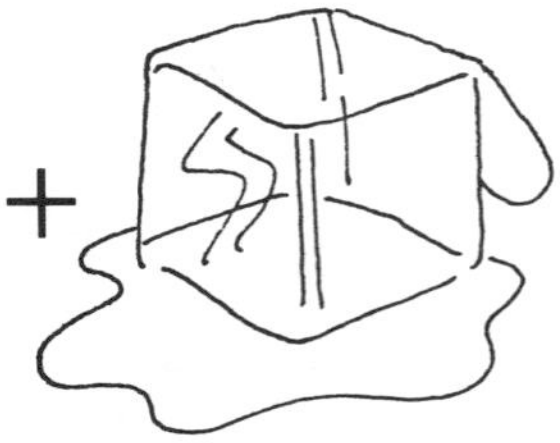 ;

______ ______

 – n

h + 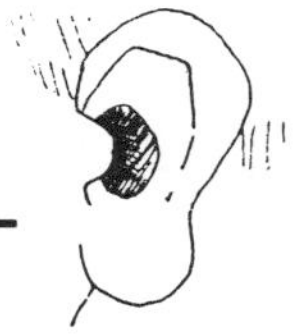 +d

______ ______

m +  – ak

 – a + y

______ ______

4  – n + rcy.

______ ______

PUZZLE #15
Proverbs 16:13

 + s t +  – c

________ ________ pleasure

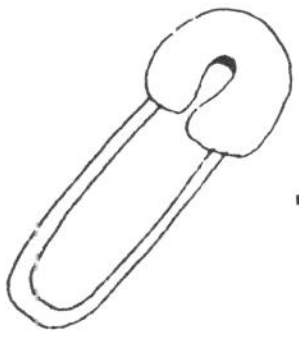 – p h + 1 + st 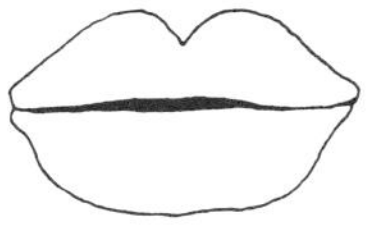 ;

____ ________ ________

t +  va + 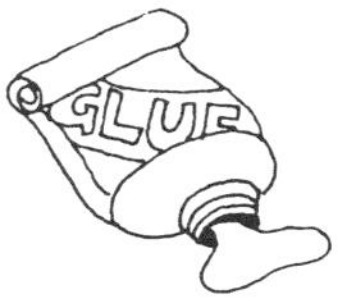

– g 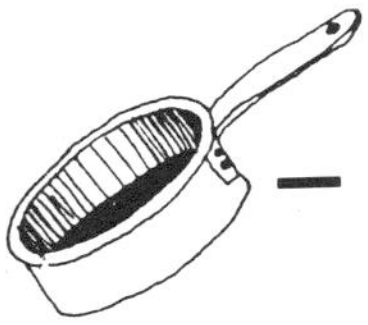 – pn 

________ ________ __ ________

w +  – use  – ou + eaks

________ ________

3 – re  – ain + uth.

________ ________

PUZZLE #16
Proverbs 3:6

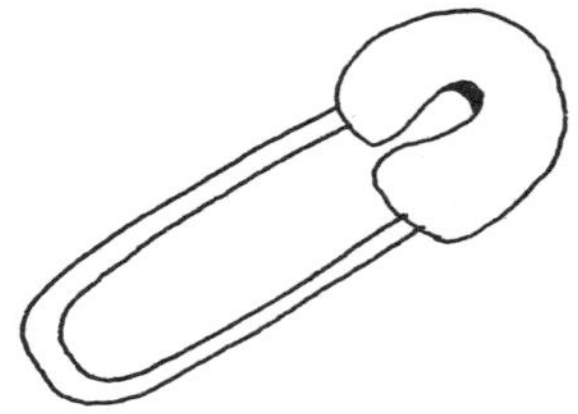 – p    – b   U + R

w +  – h + s   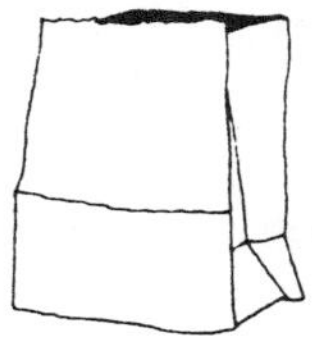 – s +nowledge

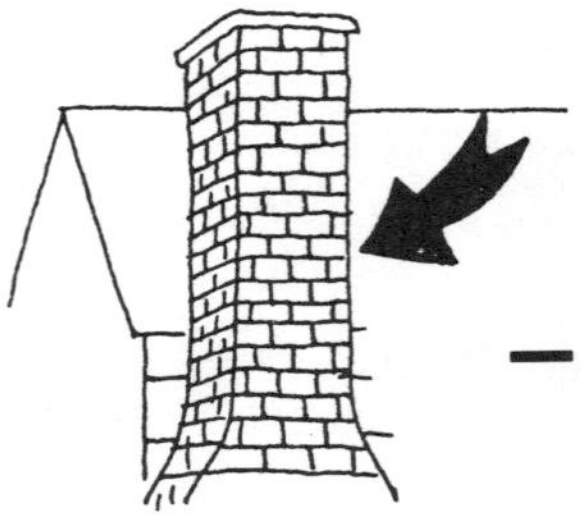 –cney,   &    – n

w +  –h   m +  –c   U + R

   st + 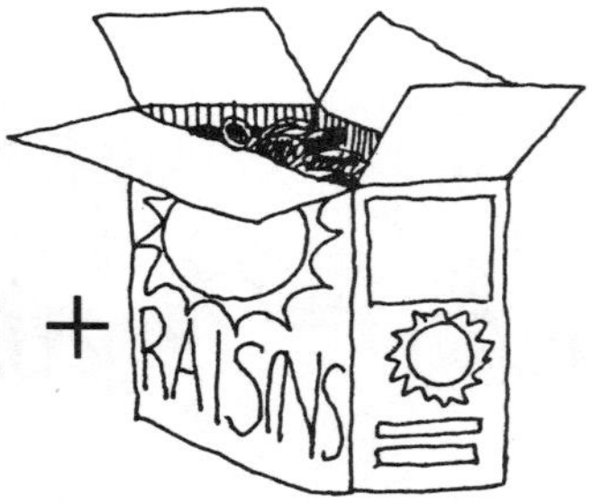

– sins + ght.

PUZZLE #17
Psalm 94:11

3 – re

k +  – s + s

______ LORD __________

3 – re

t +  – se + 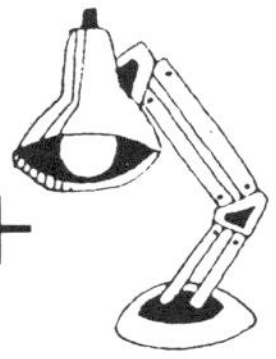 – li + s

______ ________________

of 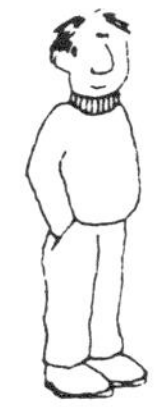 ______ ;

 – n ____

k +  – s + s

t + 

t + 

__________ ________ ________

 – c + e

 – dge + tile.

______ ____________

PUZZLE #18

Psalm 37:4

 – sk + 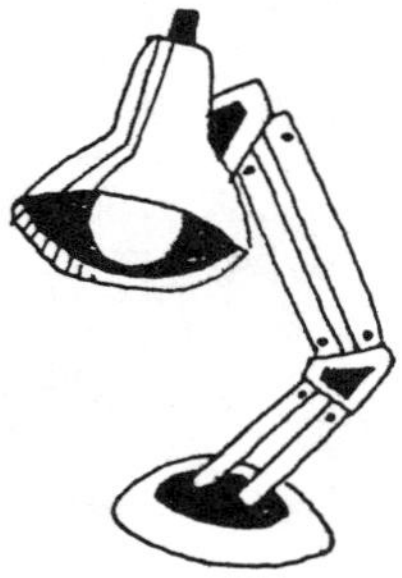

U + R + self

 – p

3 – re

&

LORD

 – n

w +  –h

gi + 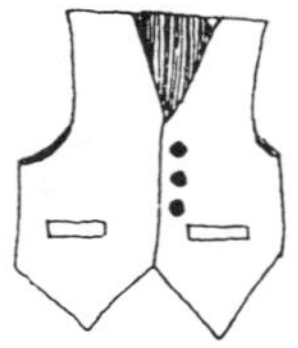 –st

3 – re

 – rs + 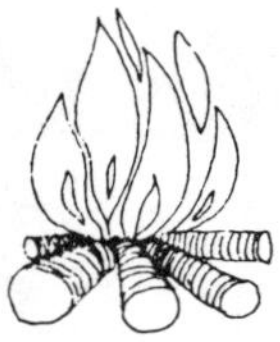 – f + s

of

U + R

 .

PUZZLE #19
Matthew 8:27

3 – re   – b + re

a +  – id + zed 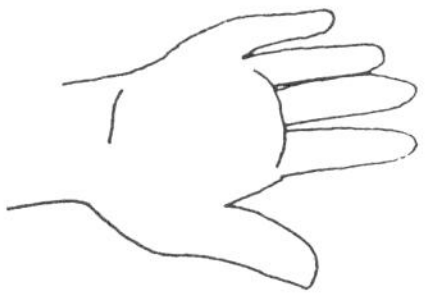 – h

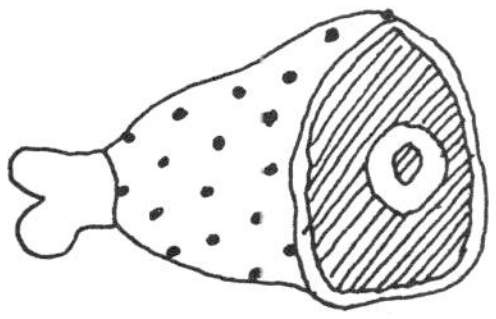 – hm + sked, “W + 

 – g + d o +  – an 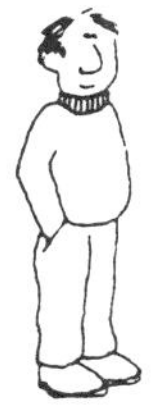

 – fh t + 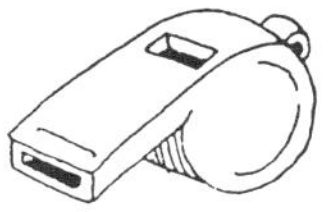 – wtle? 7–s

3 – re  – hp + nds & 3 – re

 – hle+ 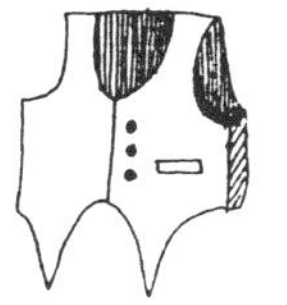 – t obey  !”

PUZZLE #20
Matthew 27:54 b

. . . t + 

______

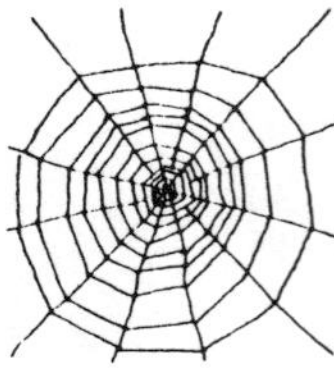 – b + re

______

terri  – r + d,

____

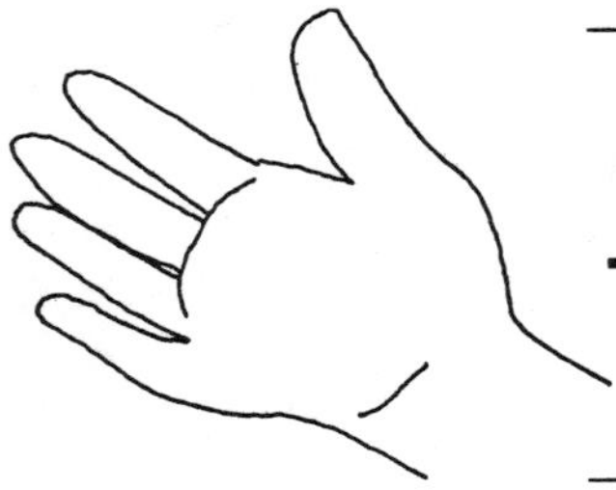 – h

____

e X + 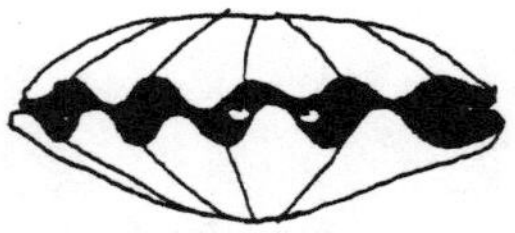 – m + imed,

____

 – n + rely

“ ________

 – n

___

 – hle + s

____

3 – re

____

____

 – sup + f

__

GOD!”

PUZZLE #21
I Chronicles 16:11

L + 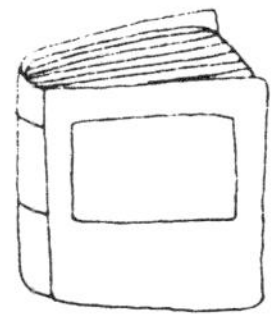 – b 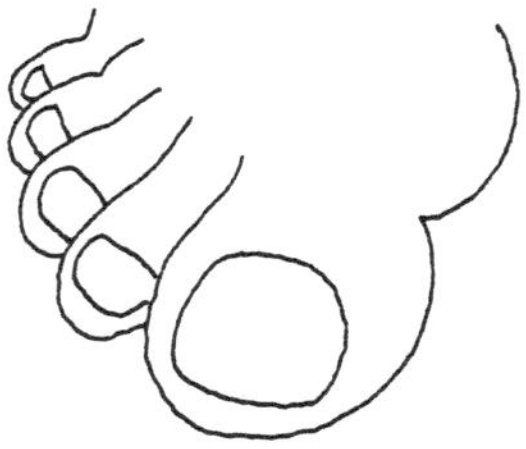 – es 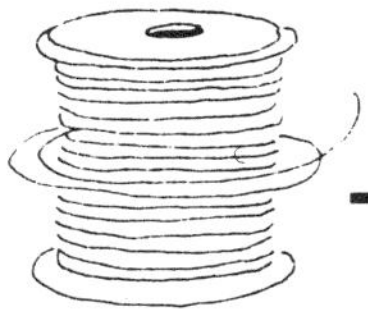 – rad

______ ______ ______

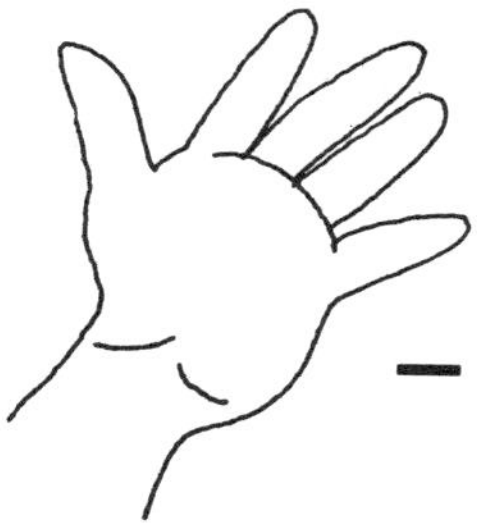 – h  – ar + s

LORD ______ ______

s +  – e + ngth;  – hp + k

______ ______

 – ar + s f + 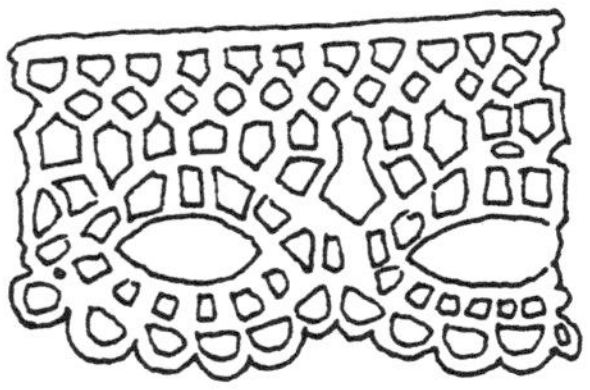 –l

______ ______

 – bl + W +  – h + S .

______

PUZZLE #22
I Chronicles 28:9 b

 – ed + rve 

". . . ________ ________ with

w + 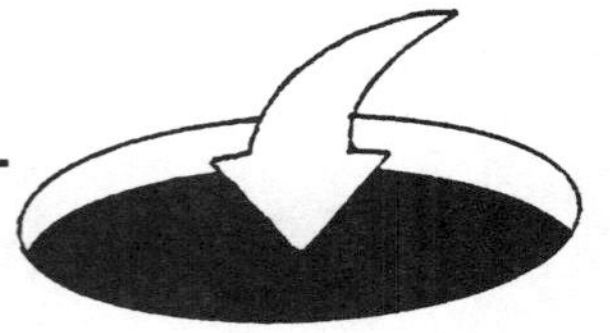 +  + ed

________________ devotion

 – h  – hp +th 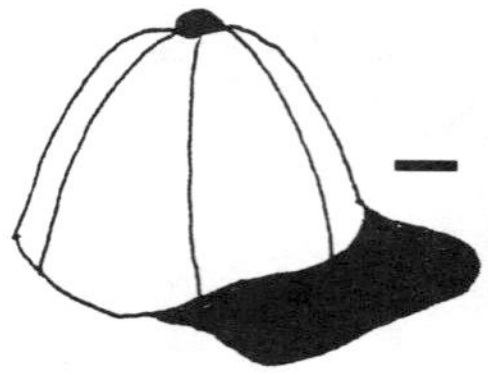 – cp

________ ________ ___

w +  + 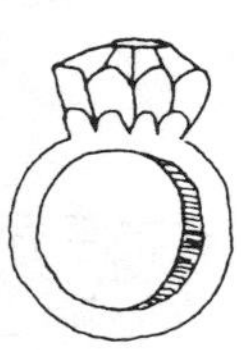 – hr  – al + nd,

________________ ________

4  – rad s + 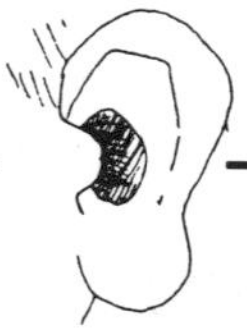 + ches

______ ______ LORD ________________

e +  – st + ry 

________________ ________ . . . ."

PUZZLE #23

I Chronicles 29:11 a

U+ R + s ,  – wl

________ ____ LORD,

 – whkers 3 – re

____ ____ greatness

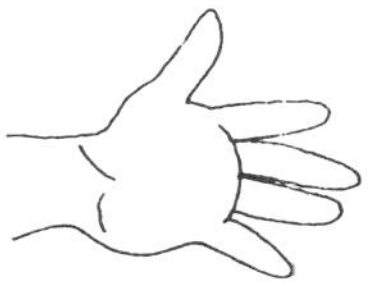 – h 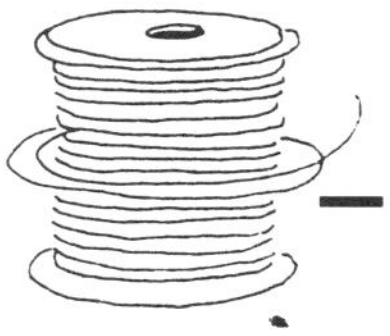 – rad p +  – – fl

____ ____ ________

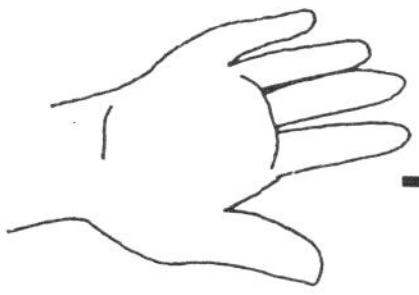 – h  – rad

____ ____

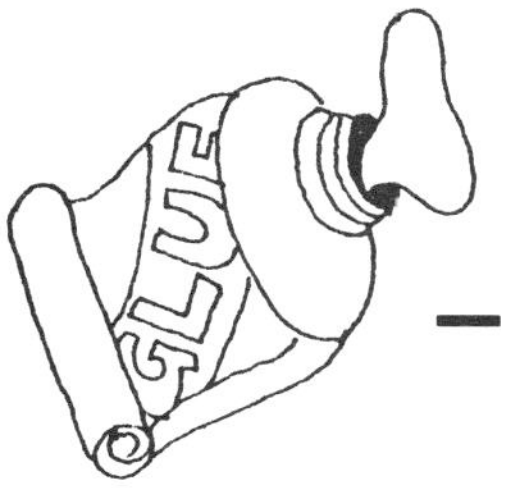

– ue + ory  – h 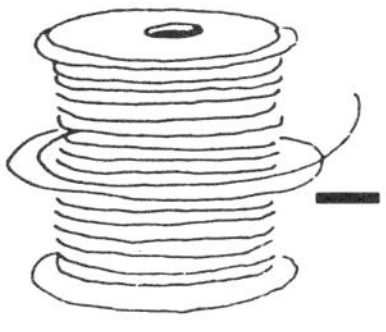 – rad

________ ____ ____

maj+  –n + y 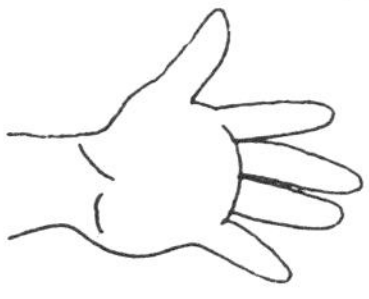 – h

________ ____

 –rad  – 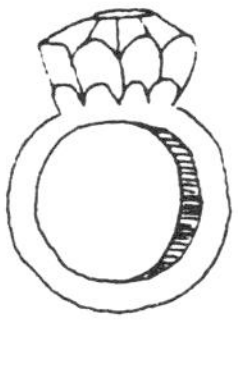 + lendor , . . .

____ ________

PUZZLE #24
Psalm 85:11

 – n + ithful +  – t + s

____

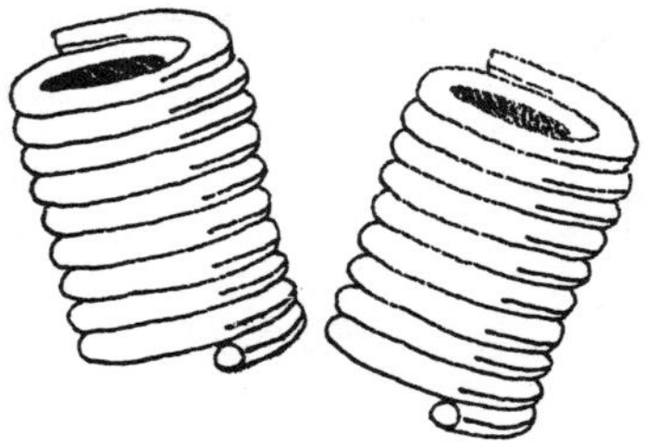 4 + th  – g + m

__________ __________ __________

3 – re  ,  – h

__________ __________ , __________

r +  – l+ e  – he + ness

____

l + 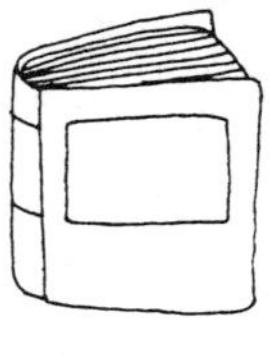 –b + s d +  – cr

__________ __________

 – g + m  – n + aven.

__________ __________

PUZZLE #25
Psalm 55:22

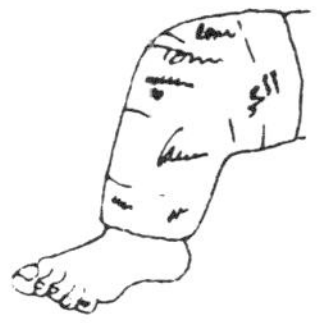 ______ U + R ______  + es ______

 – t ______ 3 – re ______ LORD

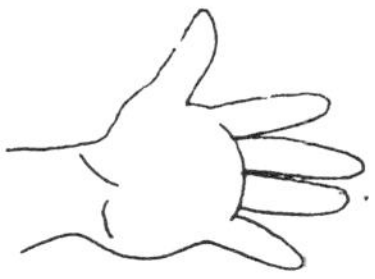 – h ______  – n ______ w +  – h ______

S+  – b +  – r ______  ______ ;

 – n ______ w +  – h ______ never l + 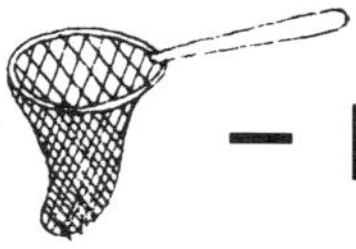 – n ______

3 – re ______ r + 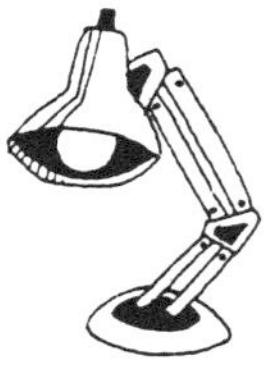 – l + eous ______ fall.

PUZZLE #26
Psalm 37:3

 – ee + ust   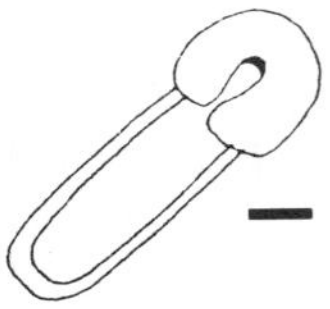 – p   3 – re

 – h    – g

LORD

 – se + d;   d +     – p

3 – re   l + 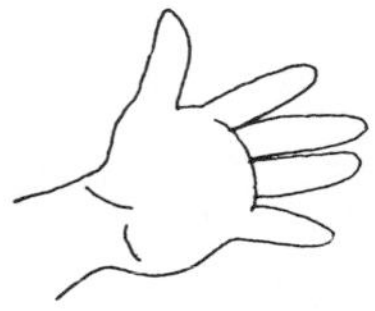 – h   &   N + joy

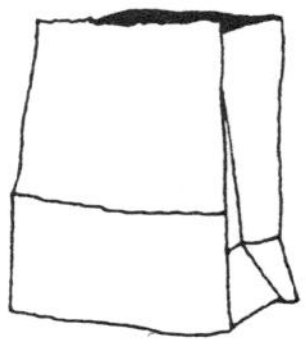 – ck + fe    – th + ture.

PUZZLE #27
Lamentations 3:25

T +  – n　　　　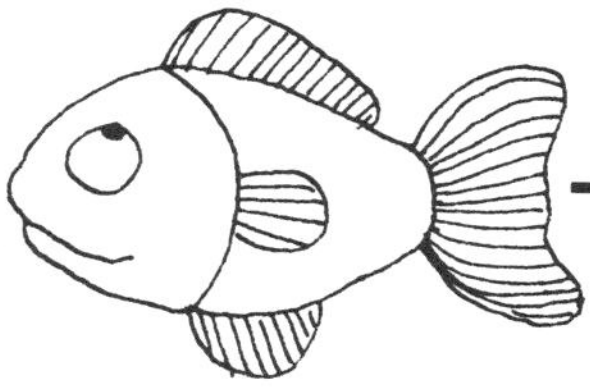 – fh

________　LORD　______

 – se + d　　2　　t + 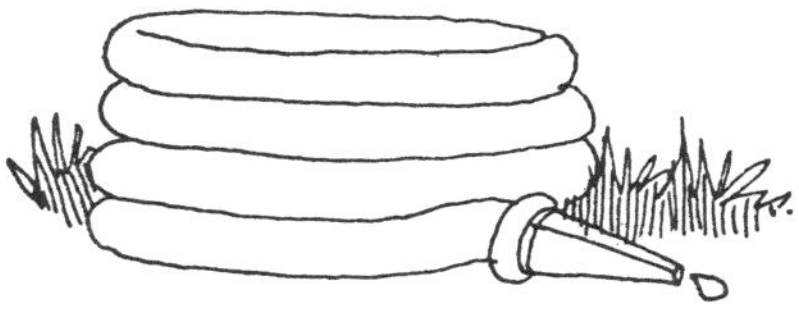

________　_____　__________

w + 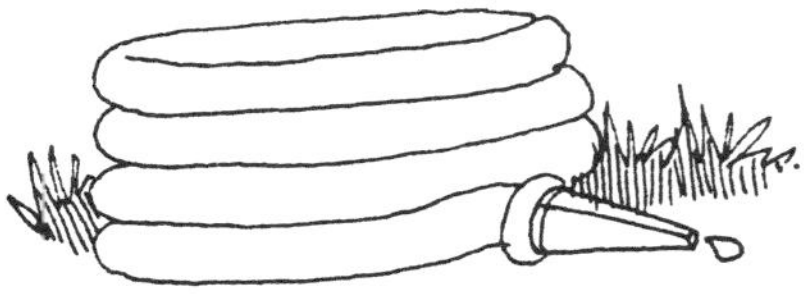　　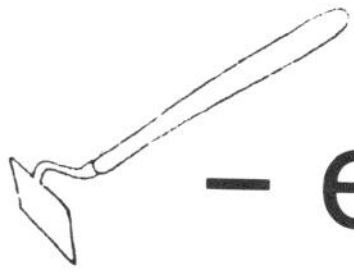 – e + 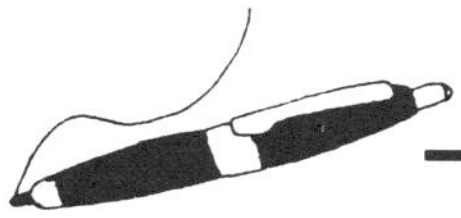 – n

__________　_________

 – fh　　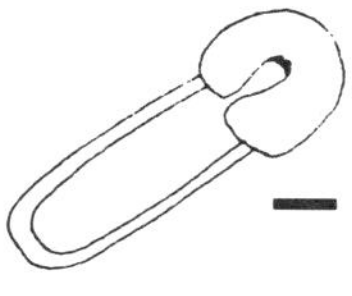 – p　　 ,　　2

______　______　_______　______

3 – re　　1　　w +  – se

______　_______　___________

 – d + ks　　 ;

_________　_______

PUZZLE #28
John 3:16

4  – up 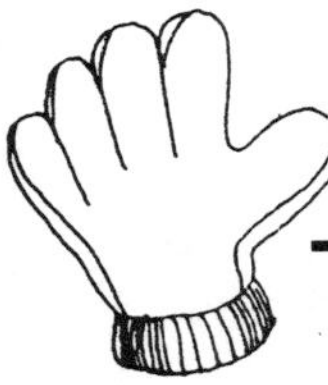 – g + d

" ______ God ______ ______

3 – re  t +   – n

______ ______ ______ ______

 – te + ve  – wtle 1 &

______ ______ ______ ______

 – t + ly  , t + 

______ ______ ______

w + 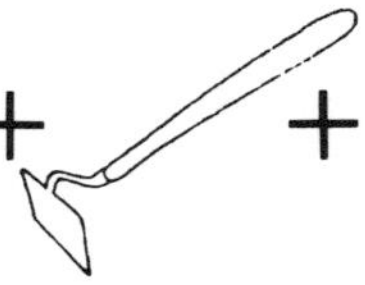 + ver  – e + lieves 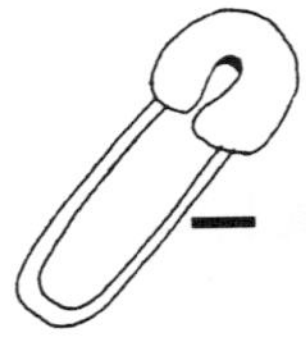 – p

______ ______ ______

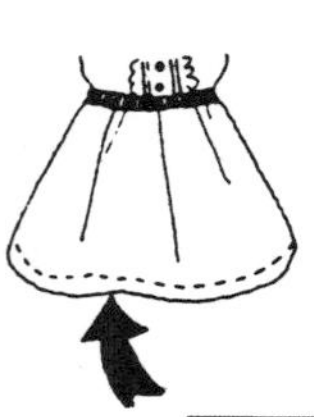 sh +  – b 

______ ______ ______ perish

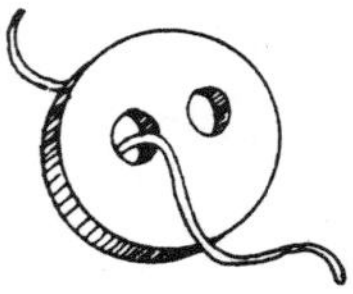 –  ½ eter + 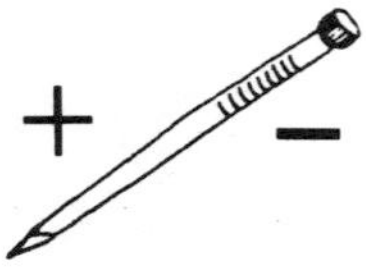 – i 

______ ______ ______ ______."

 SS886

PUZZLE #29
John 6:47, 48

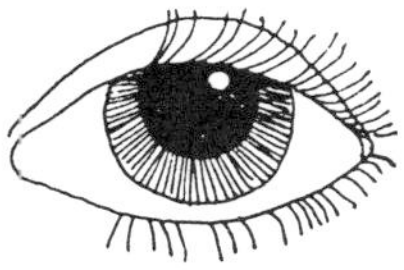

____

t +  – b

____

____

3 – re

____

 – ee + uth,

____

 – n

____

w + 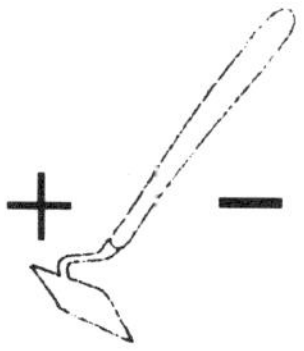 – e

____

 – e+ lieves

____

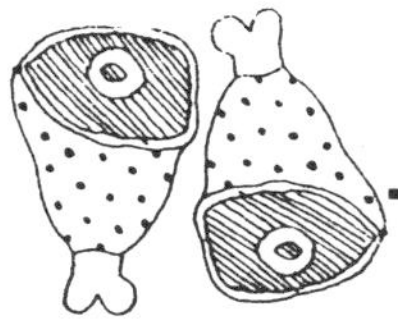 – m

____

ev + 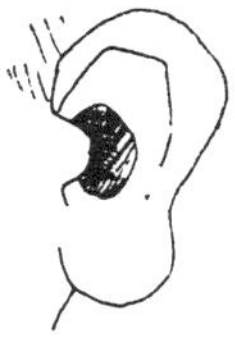 – a +last +  – k

____

.

____

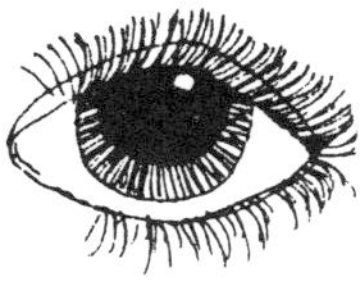

____

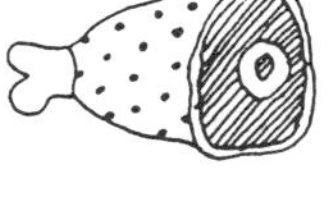 – h

____

3 – re

____

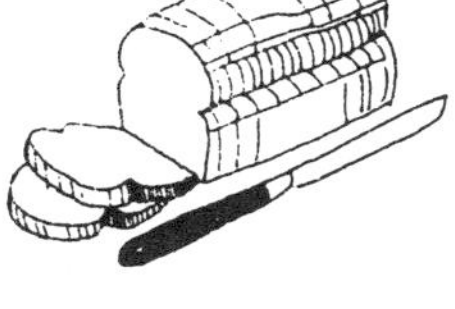

____

of

.

____

PUZZLE #30
Luke 6:37

“  – g  J +  – f, &

 w +  – h  

J +  – f + d.  – g 

 – e + demn, & U w +  – h

 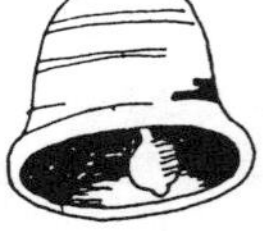 – ll  – e + demned.

4 – u + give, & 

w +  – h 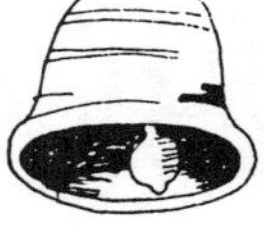 –ll 4 – u + given.”

PUZZLE #31
Luke 6:27

" 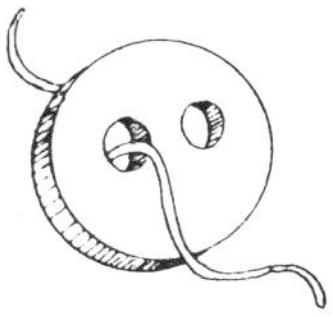 –  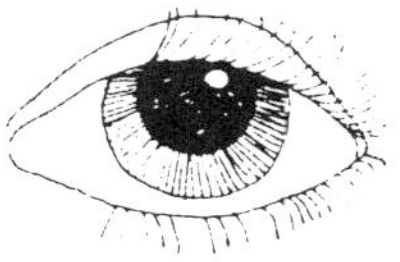 t + 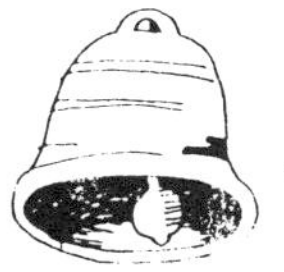 – b

______ ______ ______

 w + 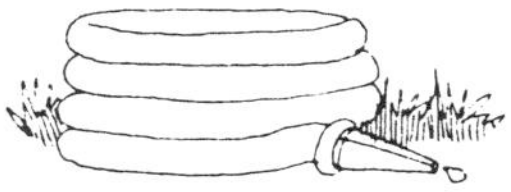 – se h + 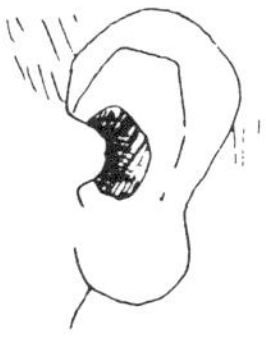

______ ______ ______

 – n : l +  – d U + R

______ ______ ______

N + M + E s,  – g  – se + d

______ ______ ______

2 t + 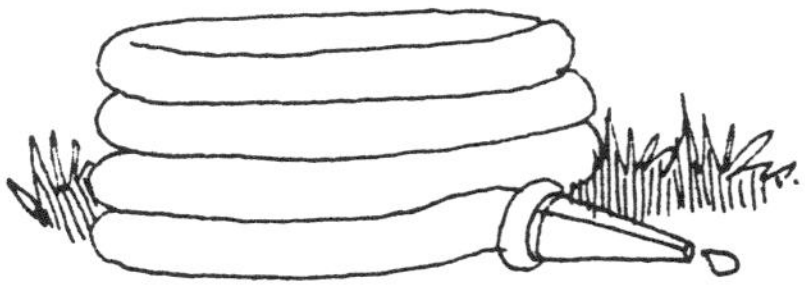 w + 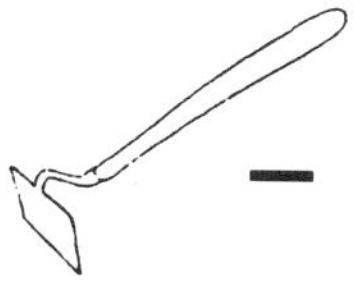 – e

______ ______ ______

h +  – g  , . . ."

______ ______

PUZZLE #32
Matthew 5:16

L + 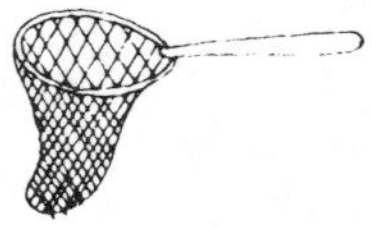 – n U + R 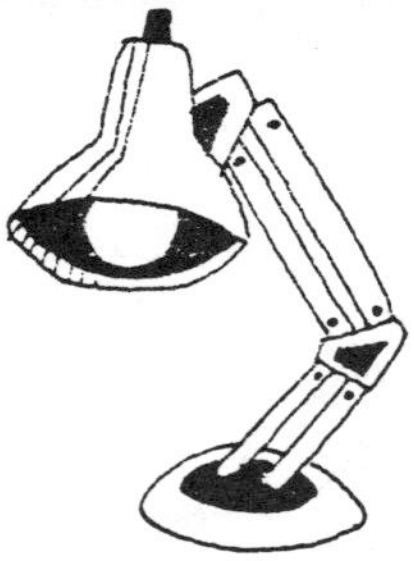

. . . ______ ______ ______

 – p + ne B + 4 

______ ______ ______ ,

t +  t +   – id +y

______ ______ ______

 – d U + R  – se +d

______ ______ ______

d +  – s + s & p + 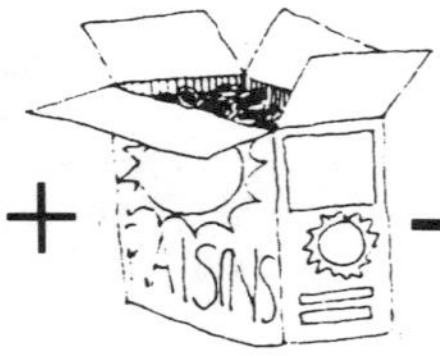 – ins + e

______ ______ ______

U + R 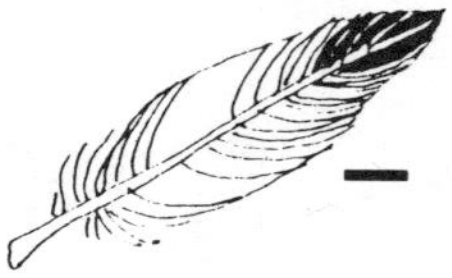 – e  – kg

______ ______ ___ heaven.

 SS886

PUZZLE #33
John 15:9

"  – gls　　3 – re　　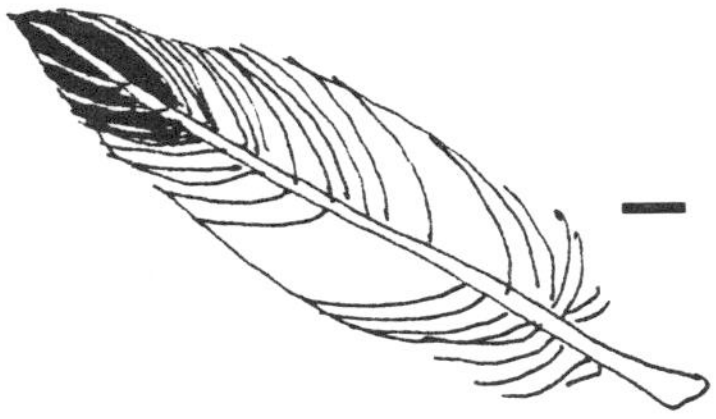 – e

________　　________　　________

h + 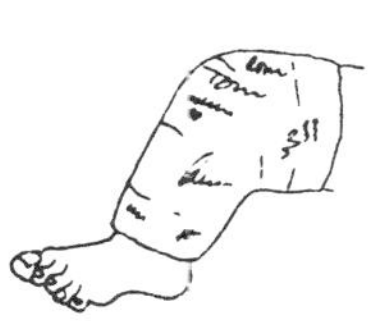 – ct　　l +  – d + d　　 – n,

________　　________　　________

 – nw　　1/2　　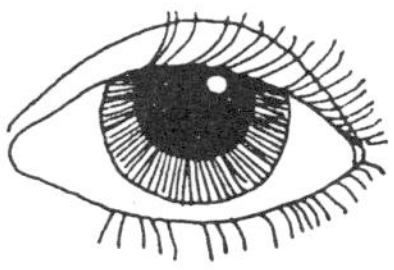

________　　________　　________

l +  – d + d　　U.　　 – s

________　　________　　________

rem +  – tr　　 – kg

________　　________

m +  – fl　　l +  – d."

________　　________

PUZZLE #34
Mark 10:27

Je +  – n + s ______

l +  – b + ed ______

 – c ______

t +  ______

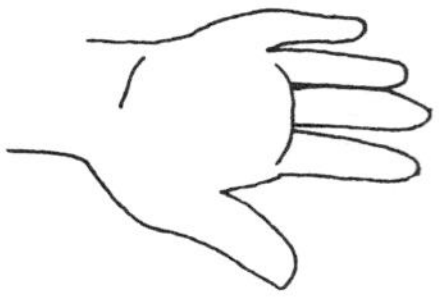 – h ______

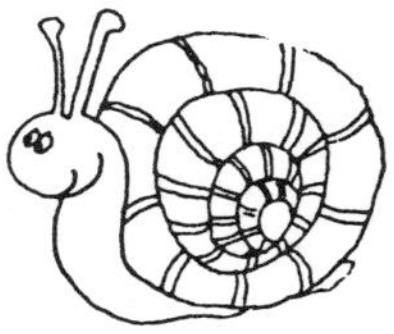 – nl + d, ______

“  – hp +th ______

 ______

t + 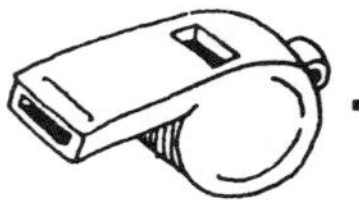 – wtle ______

 –dh ______

im +  –oum + ible , ______

 – 

______

 ______

with God;  –b ______

th +  – k + s ______

R ______  – oum + ible ______ with God.

PUZZLE #35
John 10:14

" 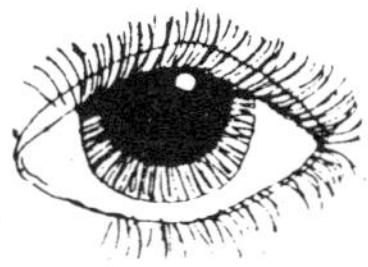 ______ 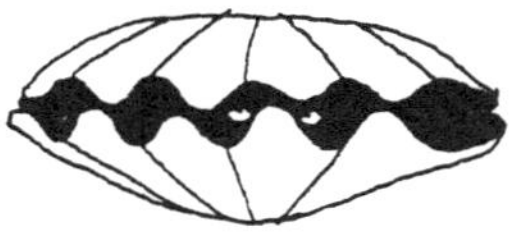 – cl ____ 3 – re ______

 – se + d ________  ________________; 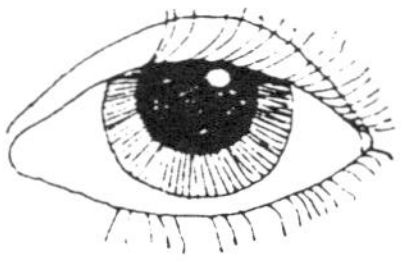 ______

k +  – s ________ m +  – fl ____

 __________ 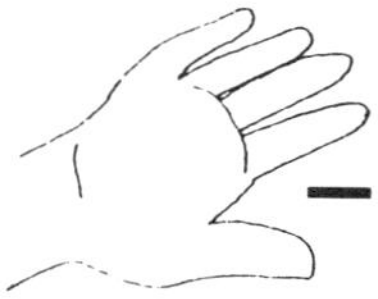 –h ______ m + 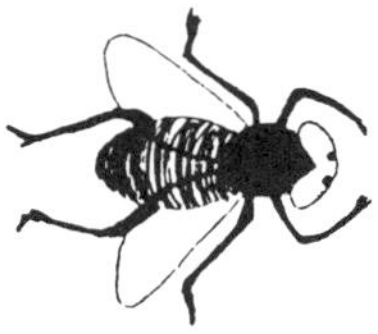 – fl ____

 __________ k +  – s ________  –n ____ ”

PUZZLE #36
Psalm 92:1

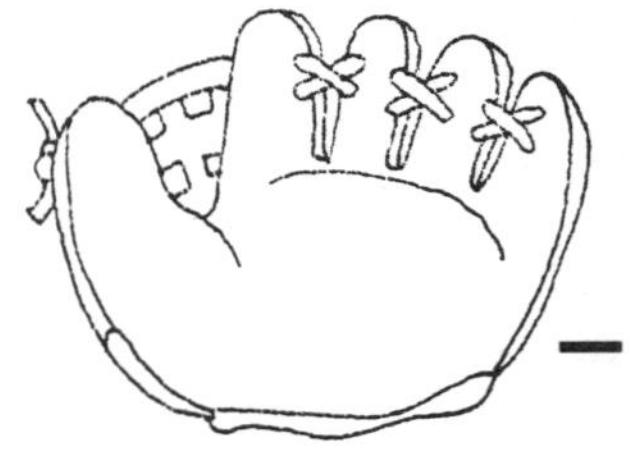 –mt    –dh    –se + d

____   ____   ________

2   p + 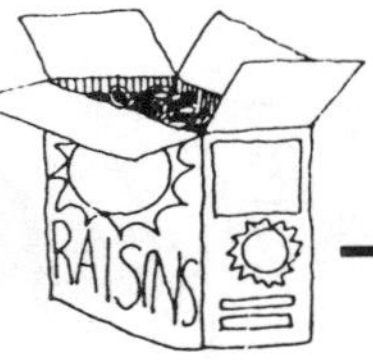 –ins + e   3 – re

______   ____________   ______

LORD   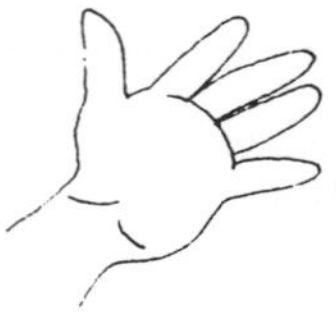 – h   m +  – c

______   ________

m +  –b+ ic   2   U + R

__________   ______   ________

n + 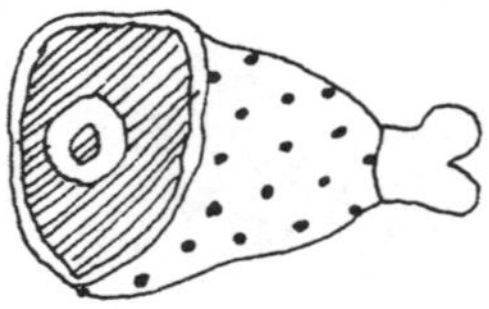 – h + e    – wl

________,   ____

Mo + 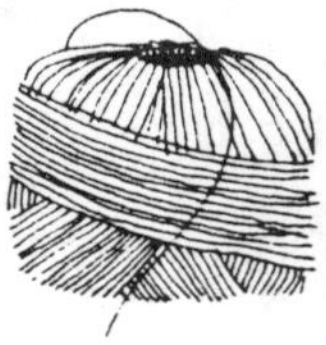 – 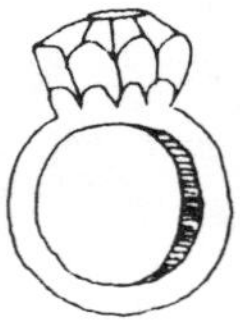   H + 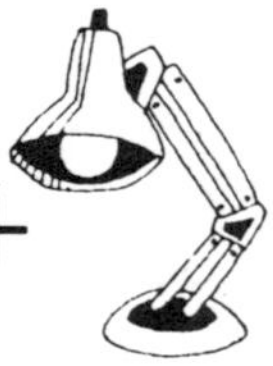 – lt

________   ________,

PUZZLE #37
Psalm 90:12

t + 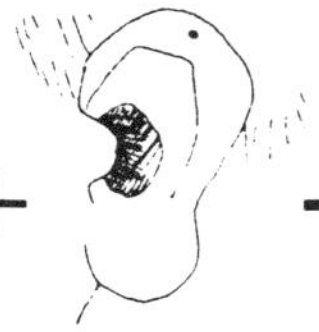 – r + ch

____

 – b

____

2

____

 – s

____

 – sp + r

____

D+ a a a a

____

ar + 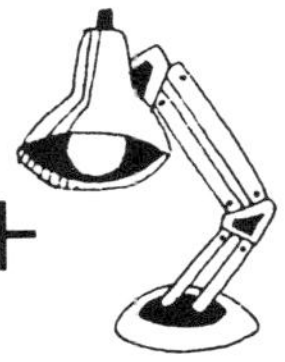 – l,

____

t + 

____

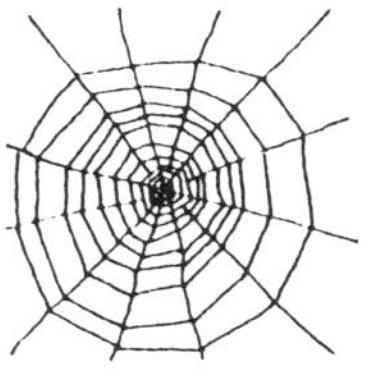 – b

____

m +  – cnd

____

g +  – tr

____

 – cn

____

____

of

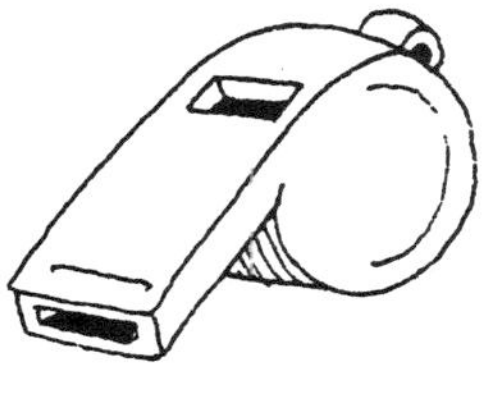 – htle + dom.

____

PUZZLE #38
Psalm 33:3

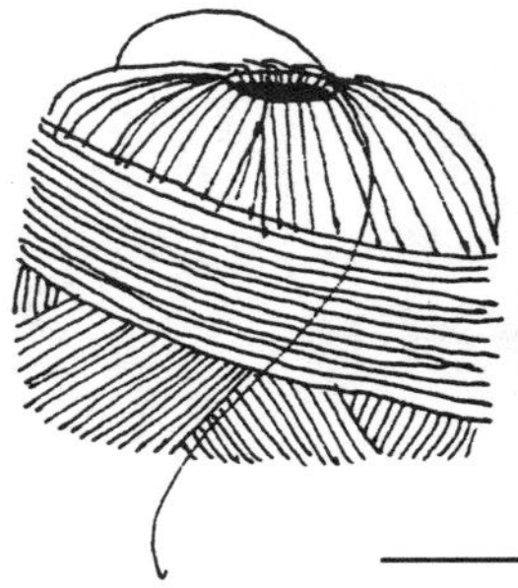 – tr ________

2 ____

 ________

 – cn ____

n +  – e ________

S + 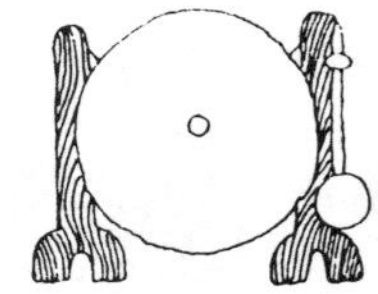 – g; ________

pl  – cnd ________

sk + 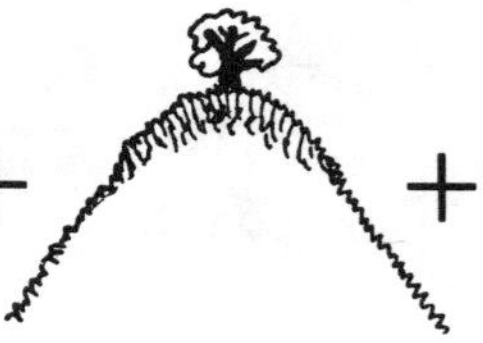 +f+  + y – hb, ____________________

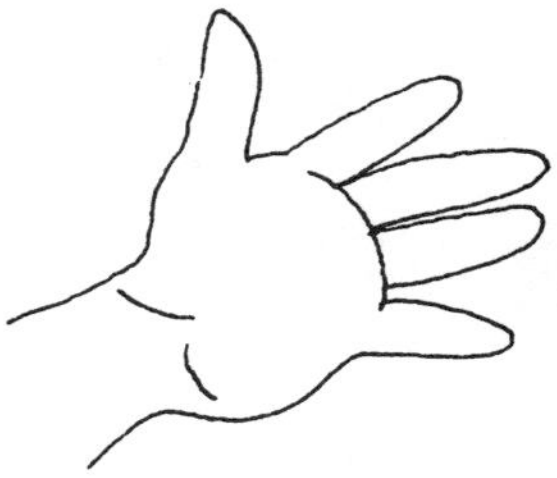 – h ________

s +  + t – se ____________

4 ________

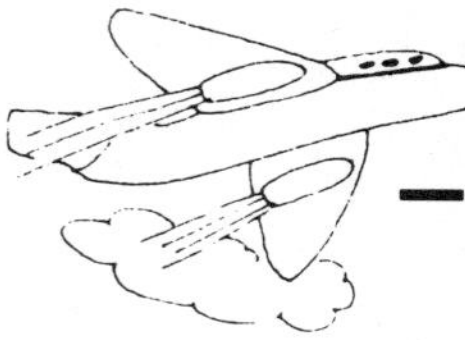 – et + oy. ________

PUZZLE #39
Matthew 28:6

 – n ______

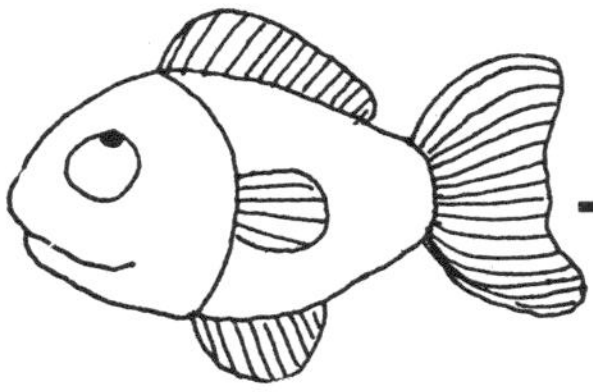 – fh ______

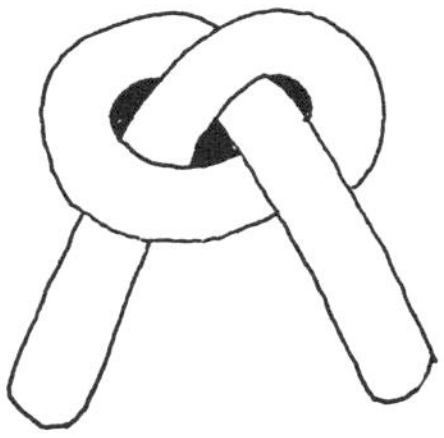 ______

 – n + re; ______

 – n ______

  – t ______

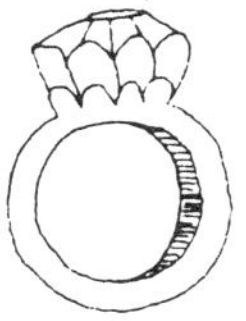 – ng + sen, ______

J +  – b + t ______

  – ht ______

he said.  – rn + me ______ & ______

 – d ______

3 – re ______

p + 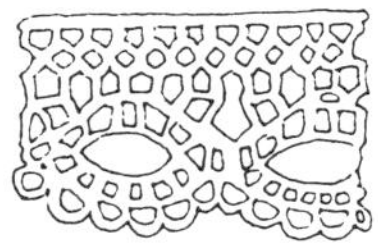 ______

w +  – n + re ______ he

l +  – cnd. ______

PUZZLE #40
Psalm 146:2

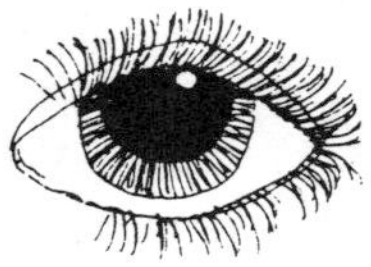 w + 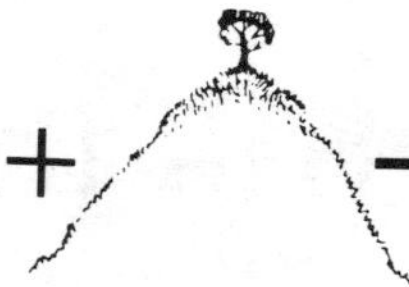 – h p + 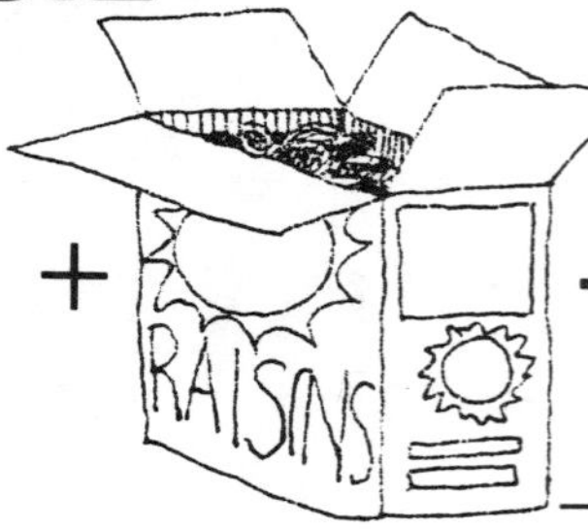 – ins + e

____ ____ ____

3 – re  – b m + 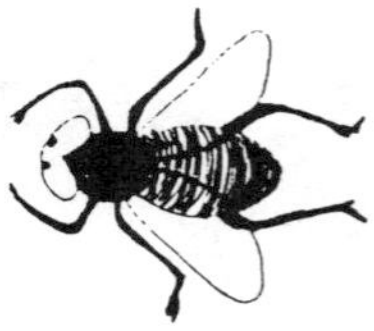 – fl

____ LORD ____ ____

 ; 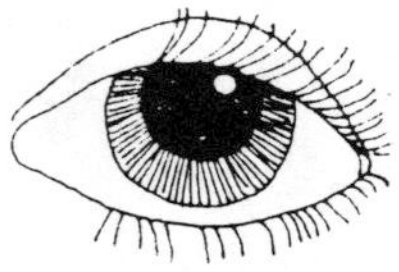 w +  –h

____ ____ ____

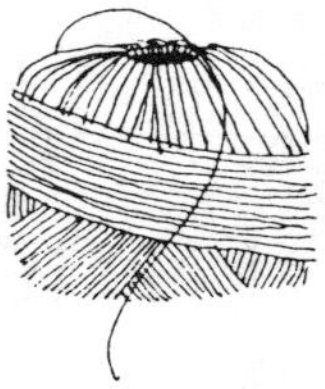 – tr p + 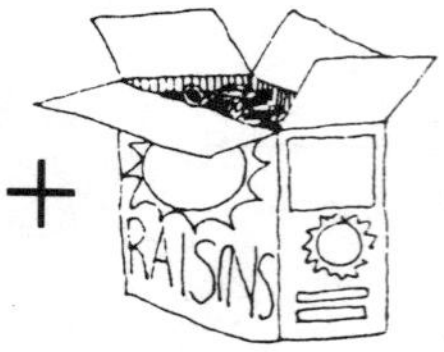 – ins + e

____ ____

2 m +  – fl

____ ____ God as

l + 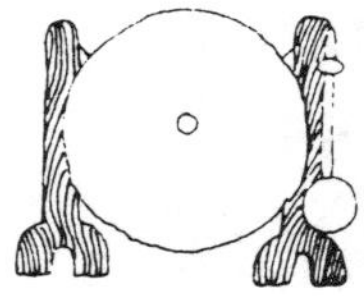 – g 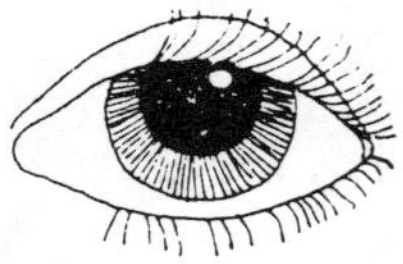 li +  – st.

____ as ____ ____

PUZZLE #41
Psalm 34:8

T + 

– p

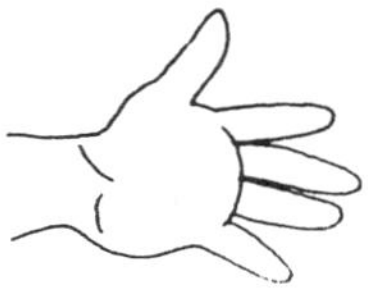 – h

– d

t +  3 – re

LORD

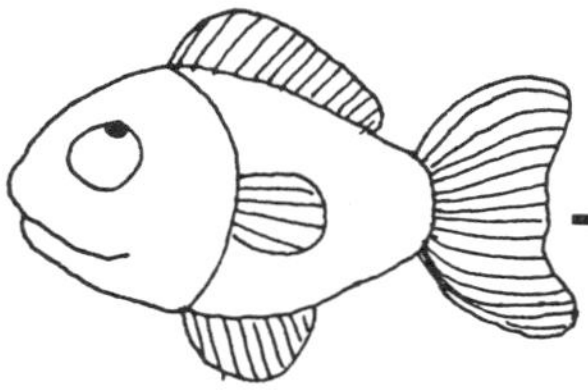 – fh

 – se + d;

bl +  – dr + ed

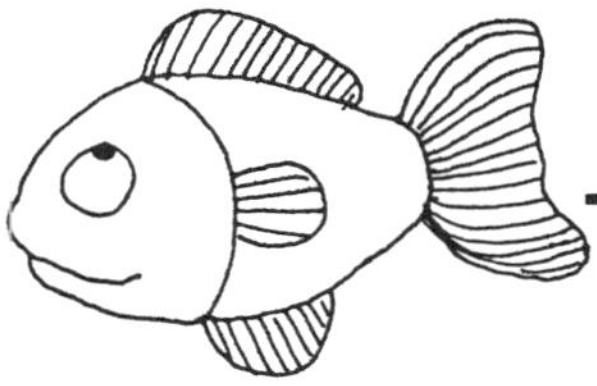 – fh

3 – re

w + 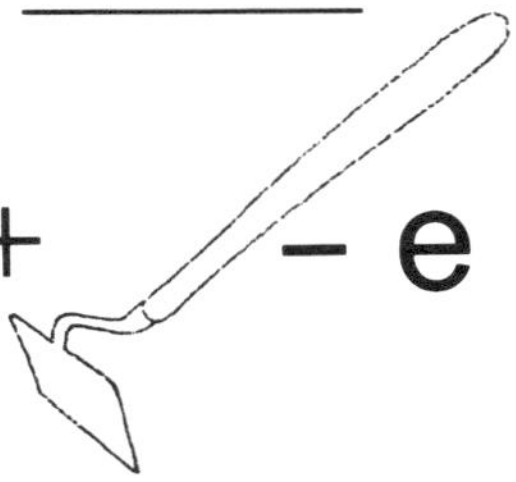 – e

t +  + s – c

re +  – d

– we

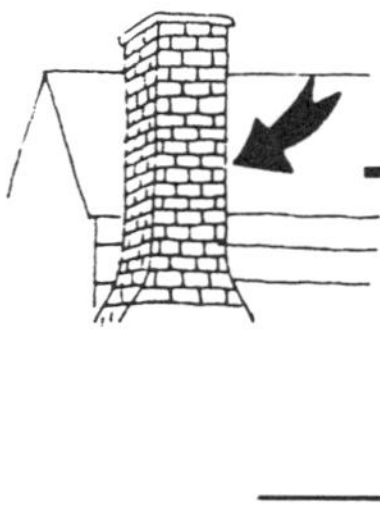 – cney.

PUZZLE #42
Luke 6:31

 – g

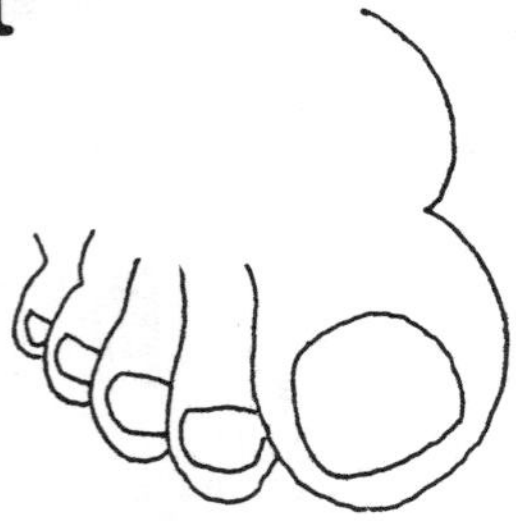 – es

O + 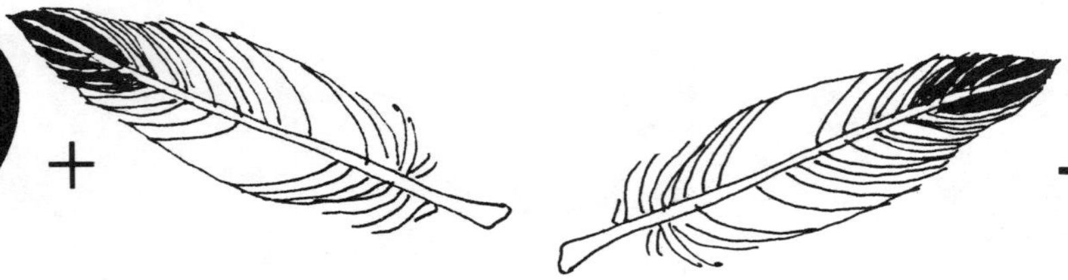 – fea

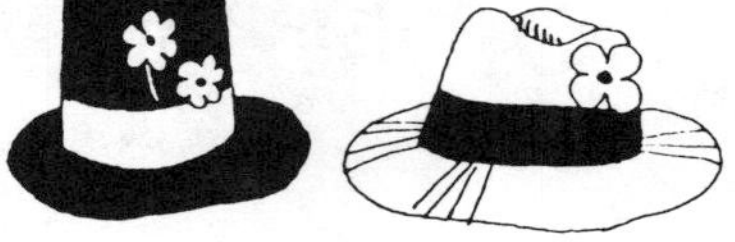 – ht

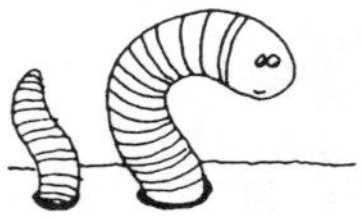 – rm + uld

1/2

t + 

 – g

2

 .

ANSWER

PUZZLE #1 p. 5
And even the very hairs of your head are all numbered.

PUZZLE #2 p. 6
Let everything that has breath praise the Lord. Praise the Lord.

PUZZLE #3 p. 7
Jesus Christ is the same yesterday and today and forever.

PUZZLE #4 p. 8
"Ask and it will be given to you; seek and you will find; knock and the door will be opened to you."

PUZZLE #5 p. 9
Surely goodness and love will follow me all the days of my life, and I will dwell in the house of the Lord forever.

PUZZLE #6 p. 10
". . . Does the clay say to the potter, 'What are you making? . . .'"

PUZZLE #7 p. 11
But the Lord is the true God; he is the living God, the eternal King."

PUZZLE #8 p. 12
In reply Jesus declared, "I tell you the truth, unless a man is born again, he cannot see the kingdom of God."

PUZZLE #9 p. 13
Jesus answered, "I am the way and the truth and the life. No one comes to the Father except through me."

PUZZLE #10 p. 14
Jesus said, "My kingdom is not of this world. If it were, my servants would fight to prevent my arrest by the Jews . . . ."

PUZZLE #11 p. 15
. . . but the gift of God is eternal life in Christ Jesus our Lord.

PUZZLE #12 p. 16
. . . I am the first and I am the last; apart from me there is no God.

PUZZLE #13 p. 17
And we know that in all things God works for the good of those who love him, who have been called according to his purpose.

PUZZLE #14 p. 18
I love the Lord, for he heard my voice; he heard my cry for mercy.

PUZZLE #15 p. 19
Kings take pleasure in honest lips; they value a man who speaks the truth.

PUZZLE #16 p. 20
in all your ways acknowledge him, and he will make your paths straight.

PUZZLE #17 p. 21
The Lord knows the thoughts of man; he knows that they are futile.

PUZZLE #18 p. 22
Delight yourself in the Lord and he will give you the desires of your heart.

PUZZLE #19 p. 23
The men were amazed and asked, "What kind of man is this? Even the winds and the waves obey him!"

PUZZLE #20 p. 24
. . . they were terrified, and exclaimed, "Surely he was the Son of God!"

PUZZLE #21 p. 25
Look to the Lord and his strength; seek his face always.

PUZZLE #22 p. 26
". . . serve him with wholehearted devotion and with a willing mind, for the Lord searches every heart . . . ."

PUZZLE #23 p. 27
Yours, O Lord, is the greatness and the power and the glory and the majesty and the splendor, . . .

PUZZLE #24 p. 28
Faithfulness springs forth from the earth, and righteousness looks down from heaven.

PUZZLE #25 p. 29
Cast your cares on the Lord and he will sustain you; he will never let the righteous fall.

PUZZLE #26 p. 30
Trust in the Lord and do good; dwell in the land and enjoy safe pasture.

PUZZLE #27 p. 31
The Lord is good to those whose hope is in him, to the one who seeks him;

PUZZLE #28 p. 32
"For God so loved the world that he gave his one and only Son, that whoever believes in him shall not perish but have eternal life."

PUZZLE #29 p. 33
I tell you the truth, he who believes has everlasting life. I am the bread of life.

PUZZLE #30 p. 34
"Do not judge, and you will not be judged. Do not condemn, and you will not be condemned. Forgive, and you will be forgiven."

PUZZLE #31 p. 35
"But I tell you who hear me: Love your enemies, do good to those who hate you, . . ."

PUZZLE #32 p. 36
. . . let your light shine before men, that they may see your good deeds and praise your Father in heaven.

PUZZLE #33 p. 37
"As the Father has loved me, so have I loved you. Now remain in my love."

PUZZLE #34 p. 38
Jesus looked at them and said, "With man this is impossible, but not with God; all things are possible with God."

PUZZLE #35 p. 39
"I am the good shepherd; I know my sheep and my sheep know me—"

PUZZLE #36 p. 40
It is good to praise the Lord and make music to your name, O Most High,

PUZZLE #37 p. 41
Teach us to number our days aright, that we may gain a heart of wisdom.

PUZZLE #38 p. 42
Sing to him a new song; play skillfully, and shout for joy.

PUZZLE #39 p. 43
He is not here; he has risen, just as he said. Come and see the place where he lay.

PUZZLE #40 p. 44
I will praise the Lord all my life; I will sing praise to my God as long as I live.

PUZZLE #41 p. 45
Taste and see that the Lord is good; blessed is the man who takes refuge in him.

PUZZLE #42 p. 46
Do to others as you would have them do to you.

 – se + d

______

 – m + k

______

2:

______ ______

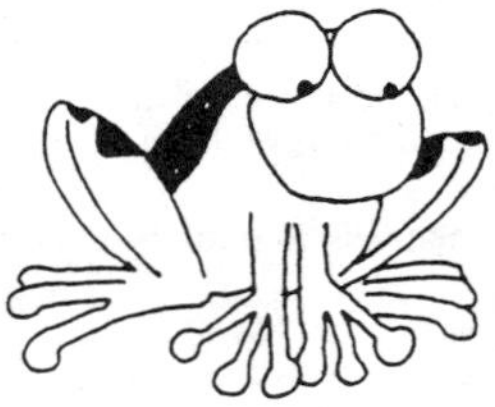 – g + m:

______ ______

Re + 

______

AWARD

TO: ______

DATE: ______

SIGNATURE: ______

Date: ______

Signature: ______

B + 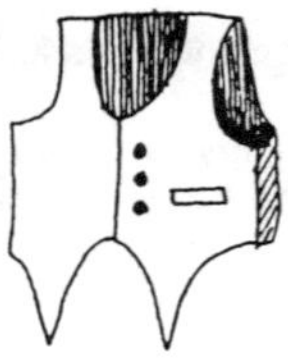 – V

______

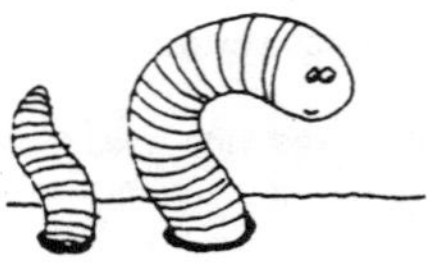 – m + ker

______

TO: ______

DATE: ______

SIGNATURE: ______